BALLET

CLASSIC *f*M
HANDY
GUIDES

BALLET

TIM LIHOREAU

First published 2015 by
Elliott and Thompson Limited
27 John Street
London WC1N 2BX
www.eandtbooks.com

ISBN: 978-1-78396-044-6

9 8 7 6 5 4 3 2 1

A catalogue record for this book is available from the
British Library.

Typesetting: Marie Doherty
Printed in the UK by TJ International Ltd

Contents

Introduction

At Classic FM, we spend a lot of our time dreaming up wonderful ways of making sure that as many people as possible across the UK have the opportunity to listen to classical music. As the nation's biggest classical music radio station, we feel that we have a responsibility to share the world's greatest music as widely as we can.

Over the years, we have written a variety of classical music books in all sorts of shapes and sizes. But we have never put together a series of books quite like this.

This set of books covers a whole range of aspects of classical music. They are all written in Classic FM's friendly, accessible style and you can rest assured that they are packed full of facts about classical music. Read separately, each book gives you a handy snapshot of a particular subject area. Added together, the series combines to offer a more detailed insight into the full story of classical music. Along the way, we shall be paying particular attention to some of the key composers whose music we play most often on the radio station, as well as examining many of classical music's subgenres.

These books are relatively small in size, so they are not going to be encyclopedic in their level of detail; there are other books out there that do that much better than we could ever hope to. Instead, they are intended to be enjoyable introductory guides that will be particularly useful to listeners who are beginning their voyage of discovery through the rich and exciting world of classical music. Drawing on the research we have undertaken for many of our previous Classic FM books, they concentrate on information rather than theory because we want to make this series of books attractive and inviting to readers who are not necessarily familiar with the more complex aspects of musicology.

For more information on this series, take a look at our website: www.ClassicFM.com/handyguides.

one
———

Preface

Mikhail Baryshnikov once said, 'No one is born a dancer. You have to want it more than anything.' Whether you agree with that or the American spiritual's view that 'All God's chillun got rhythm!', one thing is certain: ballet is the artistic pinnacle of dance.

When a human hears rhythmic music, it's a primal instinct to start drumming fingers or tapping feet. Studies of sleeping newborns show that they have innate rhythm. Varying rhythms were played as they slept; irregular beats caused imitative reactions in their brains, while regular motifs soothed the breast, leading scientists to conclude that we are born with a built-in sense of rhythm – possibly adopted from the mother's heart. But do we have an innate desire for *dance*?

Dance does seem to be an *instinct*. Scientists studying the brain have identified corresponding areas of the brain that are responsible for speech production and hand and leg gestures, suggesting that movements were used as a form of expression.

Put simply, *dance* may have been an early form of language.

Taking this as a starting point, it is not surprising that dance has been part of our societies for thousands of years. The Bhimbetka rock shelters, for example, in what is now Madhya Pradesh in India are thought to date back to 9000 BCE and show representations of communal dance, while an ancient Greek terracotta statuette (c. 3000 BCE) showing a woman dancing was found in Taranto, the birthplace of the dance we now call the tarantella.

All of this is dance, certainly. But it's not ballet. To find the earliest twitchings of ballet, we only have to go back to much more recent times.

two

A Brief History of Ballet

Beginnings of Ballet

As with several other forms of artistic expression that combine elements of a number of arts, it is not easy to pinpoint the moment when ballet became identifiable as a discipline in its own right.

Entertainments involving movement to music, often with over-the-top input from scene painters and costume makers, had been taking place in the courts of Europe, particularly in France and Italy, from the time of Catherine de' Medici in the mid-sixteenth century. The form, which was known as *ballet de cour*, came into its own in France, notably at the Burgundian court. It bore some relationship to the *entremets* of the fourteenth and fifteenth centuries – no, not tasty snacks 'between courses' beloved of stylish cooks today, but ever more lavish theatrical spectacles staged during banquets and portraying such events as the capture of Jerusalem or the fall of Constantinople.

Frankly, it was a bit of a ragbag. A typical *ballet de cour* might involve a song to start off with, some rhymed verses, a series of dances on a single theme (known as an *entrée*), followed by an exuberant *grand ballet* finale. Ducs and comtes, keen to demonstrate their wealth, refinement and artistic sensibility, would not only assemble the necessary talent to commission their own *ballet de cour*, but would often take a dancing role themselves. Even the Sun King himself, Louis XIV, would perform in one every now and then.

A seminal moment in the history of dance is the establishment in March 1661 in France of the Académie Royale de Danse – a first attempt to lay down some rules for the genre and prevent it developing into an even more random and bastardised form. Thirteen experts in dance were tasked by the King 'to restore the art of dancing to its original perfection and to improve it as much as possible'. The majority of the *académistes*, drawn from the King's entourage, were mostly both dancers and musicians, which demonstrates how intertwined the skills related to making music and moving to it were at the time. Indeed a document entitled 'The Marriage of Music and Dance' survives from 1664.

The founding of the Académie Royale de Danse was soon followed by the establishment of the Académie Royale de Musique. Although the two groups never formally merged, many members of both committees were associated with the Paris Opera Ballet, and over time the dancers – at this period exclusively male – recruited to entertain the King were interchangeable with those of the stage company.

Rather than existing as an art form on its own, ballet during this period often seemed to be a discrete unit within other entertainments, such as plays and operas.

Pierre Beauchamp (1631–1705) was born into a family of dance masters. He taught Louis XIV dance for twenty-two years and before his involvement with the Académie Royale de Danse – he was Director from 1671 – he had been the principal choreographer for Molière's company of actors, the Troupe du Roy, providing the integrated ballets for plays such as *Le bourgeois Gentilhomme* and

Le Malade imaginaire. Not only is he one of the first identifiable choreographers, but he is also known as one of the first people to attempt to notate dance; his system, published by Raoul-Auger Feuillet, is known as Beauchamp–Feuillet notation. He is credited with codifying the five positions of the feet – still the basis of every child's introduction to classical ballet. He is also important to our story because of his collaborations with the composer Jean-Baptiste Lully (1632–1687).

From 1672 onwards, the calibre of Lully's music was one of the key factors in ballet's popularity. He knew his market, and his market was, in the first and most important instance, the King. Lully always reserved a place in his operas and *tragédies en musique* for substantial danced sections. If the King was a fan of ballet, then Lully, the Italian servant made good, was canny enough to ensure that there was always ballet for Beauchamp to choreograph and for the King to enjoy.

The Beauchamp–Feuillet publication *Choreography, or The Art of Notating Dance* gives us some inkling of what these ballets looked like. Performed exclusively by male dancers until 1681, this was movement in the service of a story. It was a language of gesture, which partly continued into the realm of the great nineteenth-century Romantic ballets, and it was enlivened by the virtuoso technique required for pirouettes and ornamented steps.

Ballet was thriving elsewhere in Europe. In Italy, which had experienced a parallel development in *ballet de cour*, ballets were now staged as interval entertainments, particularly in Venice.

In England, Charles II had been restored to the throne in 1660. After the restrictions on public performance, London looked to France for entertainment and cheerfully adopted French practice, even inviting Robert Cambert, whose *Pomone* was the first ever opera in French and who had been dislodged at the Académie by Lully, to set up a French-style Royal Academy of Music. Other musicians and dancers followed, joining and influencing English companies. The translation of the French notation books into English was a further factor in the reach and popularity of the French ballet tradition.

At his Cockpit Theatre in Drury Lane the actor Thomas Betterton staged a number of semi-operas (a mixture of spoken drama, song, dance, stage machinery and lavish spectacle) with extended ballet sections. He managed to procure the services of

Henry Purcell and Jeremiah Clarke to write music for his company. Chief among his successes was Purcell's *The Fairy Queen*, for which the Act III dances were choreographed by the Holborn-based dancing master Josias Priest. Semi-opera as a genre, however, ran into the buffers at the turn of the seventeenth century when the Lord Chamberlain decreed that plays without music and the new genre of Italian opera should be licensed as separate entities.

French influence could be felt throughout western Europe, in Dresden, Hamburg and in Sweden. Lully's personal popularity was widespread, and enjoyment of the French style of incorporating danced sections within other genres was to lead to local commissions. By the time of his death in 1687 he was no longer enjoying the King's patronage to the extent he once had – scandal surrounding his dissolute personal life had driven him from favour and the King snubbed him publicly by not inviting him to conduct his opera *Armide* at Versailles. However, the status of ballet was assured and its popularity did not depend solely on the reputation of the composer who had done so much to establish it.

Enter *Opéra-ballet*

The next development was the genre of *opéra-ballet*, as dance elements became embedded into the narrative structure of opera, rather than providing complementary distraction during opera performances. The emergence of this new genre is usually dated from the composition of André Campra's *L'Europe galante* in 1697. While modelled on the *entrée* section of the *ballet de cour*, taking the expression of love as its theme over four acts, this work pulled together the sung and danced elements in an equal partnership.

Ballet was still growing in popularity for providing interludes in drama. It was flourishing as both a vehicle for narrative and as an abstract entertainment-within-an-entertainment in both theatres and opera houses with more and more dancers being employed across the continent. And the popularity of dance was beginning to make stars of dancers such as Jean Balon (1676–1739), who appeared in *Les Horaces* (see page 10) and Marie Anne de Cupis de Camargo (1710–1770), dubbed 'La Camargo'. Hailing from Brussels, she made her name with a signature move, a foursome of rapid crossed steps (*the entrechat quatre*); such was her fame, French restaurants names dishes after her, like the Bombe Camargo and the Soufflé Camargo.

Ballet was about to become a complete entertainment in its own right and not as an appendage – although an increasingly dominant appendage – to drama and opera.

Total Ballet

There are two contenders to be the first complete ballet. In 1714 the Duchesse du Maine commissioned two principal dancers from l'Opéra, Jean Balon and Françoise Prévost, to present an entertainment based on the final act of a tragedy by Pierre Corneille, *Les Horaces*. There was no singing, no speech, simply dance and mime to music. The Duchesse's guests, the intellectual elite of the day, gathered in the intimate setting of Château de Sceaux on the Île de France, were said to be deeply moved, some weeping at Prévost's performance, lamenting the death of her lover at the hands of her brother. However, this was a *private* performance and some would therefore discount it as the first true fully staged ballet.

The first public performance of a ballet took place on 2 March 1717 not in France or Italy but at

London's Drury Lane Theatre. English choreographer John Weaver (1673–1760) produced *The Loves of Mars and Venus,* with French star Louis Dupré (known as *'le dieu de la danse'*, having performed at the Paris Opera for more than thirty-five years, well into his sixties) and English ballerina Hester Santlow as the lovers and Weaver himself as Vulcan. It made such an impact that it inspired a parody version by John Rich, the impresario behind John Gay's *The Beggar's Opera*.

Weaver followed this up a year later with *Orpheus and Eurydice,* 'a dramatick entertainment in dancing therupon'. He was responsible for a translation of the Beauchamp–Feuillet notation book and tried to set up a school of 'pantomime' – not the Christmas entertainment we think of today but a style of narrative movement, both heroic and emotional. It was an uphill struggle – in 1730 he was complaining about the public preference for 'pseudo-players, merry-andrews, tumblers and rope-dancers'.

With the advent of a concern for dramatic truth and narrative structure in ballet, established composers, who had up to this point provided music for danced interludes, became involved in the conception of works far more reliant on dance. Marie Sallé, a trail-blazing dancer and choreographer, who leant towards expressive, dramatic performances rather than concentrating on virtuoso display, collaborated with both Handel and Gluck. And Jean-Philippe Rameau had a great success with *Les Indes galantes*, an *opéra-ballet*, in 1735. Ten years earlier French settlers in the New World had sent six Native American chiefs to Paris, where they met Louis XV, pledged allegiance to the crown and presented three kinds of dances at the Théâtre-Italien. This provided Rameau with the inspiration for the fourth of his four *entrées*, *Les Sauvages*.

Complete ballets, half-and-half *opéra-ballets*, and ballets as interludes in drama and opera continued for some time side by side. It was Jean-Georges Noverre (1727–1810) who caught the zeitgeist and formulated and furthered the *ballet d'action*, where character and emotion were the driving forces. He concentrated on conveying feeling through the dancers' bodies and faces rather than focusing on technical expertise. He worked in Paris, Berlin, Dresden, Strasburg, Lyons and London, where the actor-manager David Garrick referred to him as 'the Shakespeare of the dance'. He could count among his friends Voltaire, Mozart and Frederick the Great. His birthday, 29 April, is now observed as International Dance Day.

Gluck, the bringer of emotional realism to opera with his reforms to *opera seria*, offered the same service to ballet. His *Don Juan*, with choreography by the Italian dancer, choreographer and composer Gaspere Angiolini, opened in Vienna in 1761. In 1766 Angiolini became Director of the Imperial Theatre in St Petersburg, taking the *ballet d'action* to Russia.

By the end of the eighteenth century, there was an enormous public appetite for ballet. Throughout Europe and increasingly beyond, opera houses, which were still providing a home for ballet in its own right and as part of opera performance, were enlarging their companies – the Paris Opera had nearly a hundred dancers on its books at this time.

Ballet was now not a million miles from what we would recognise today on the stage of the Royal Opera House or the Bolshoi Theatre.

Romantic and Classical Ballet

In music, the eras of Classical and Romantic come in that order: Classical (1750-ish onwards) and then Romantic (1830-ish onwards). In ballet, these eras are reversed, although with very different date ranges. Romantic ballet came first, in the early to mid-nineteenth century, while what we now term 'classical ballet' had its golden age in the late nineteenth century, overlapping into the twentieth. Both, it should be said, are still very evident on ballet stages today.

Romantic ballet was muscular, almost gymnastic, for the male dancers, while the ballerinas were almost ethereal creatures, weightless, and seeming to float in the air. For plots, choreographers often turned to folklore and legend, set to music written by the greatest composers of the day. Special effects – for instance, the 'limelight' produced by gas lighting – began to be commonplace, and ballet 'skirts' were widely adopted alongside tutus. This was the period of *ballet blanc*, where the stage was an ocean of white skirts and bodices. The three decades from Adam's *Giselle* in 1841 to Delibes' *Coppélia* in 1870 saw Romantic ballet at its height.

Ballets were still very much in evidence in the world of opera as well. A glance at the big operas of the day reveals sometimes overlooked ballet gems. The *Pas de cinq* in Weber's *Euryanthe*; the meaty dance scenes in Glinka and Rossini (*William Tell*, for instance, which contained two big scenes for Italian-Swedish dancer Marie Taglioni). Wagner came a cropper when he riled the influential Jockey Club by *not* putting the requisite ballet in his opera, *Tannhäuser*, at its Paris premiere in 1861, provoking a riot.

Ballet's innovations were spreading around the world. The choreographer Auguste Bournonville moved from Paris back to his native Danish Court and began to produce a huge body of work there, but the one crucial place on the ballet circuit, which would begin to grow and grow, was Russia.

Jules Perrot, the French ballet master who had made his name in London and Naples, made the move to become the Ballet Master at the Imperial Ballet in St Petersburg, followed by the choreographer of *Coppélia*, Arthur Saint-Léon. Together with the Bolshoi in Moscow (originally founded as an orphanage by Catherine the Great) the two companies would pave the way for a Russian dominance of ballet, enforced by the collaboration of its greatest composer: Tchaikovsky.

How *did* the Russians come to dominate the classical ballet scene? It is probably through the combined efforts of two masters in their field: the choreographer Marius Petipa and the composer Pyotr Ilyich Tchaikovsky. Their collaboration on *Swan Lake* (1877) caught the public imagination and St Petersburg was plastered with posters for *The Sleeping Beauty* (1890) and *The Nutcracker* (1892) long before they were in rehearsal. Petipa was responsible for nearly fifty original ballets – core repertoire for Russian companies ever since. When Petipa fell ill during the preparation of *The Nutcracker*, his younger colleague Lev Ivanov took over. Ivanov was to become almost as influential as Petipa.

20th Century Rocks

Possibly the most influential figure in ballet at the turn of the twentieth century was not a dancer or a choreographer or a composer, but an impresario, a 'fixer' *par excellence*. Serge Diaghilev brought creative artists in different fields together and thereby changed the face of dance. He became involved with ballet almost by chance. After studying law and music in St Petersburg and working on the influential arts magazine *Mir Iskusstva* he conceived the idea of assembling a troupe of performers and heading to Paris with a show – not a ballet but an

opera, Borodin's *Prince Igor*. As he could not afford
to stage the complete opera, he took only the second act. This act included the dance set-piece, the
Polovtsian Dances, stunningly choreographed by
Ivanov. The Parisian audience in 1909 might have
liked the opera – but they *loved* the ballet.

So the Ballet Russes was born, complete with
a new genius choreographer, Michel Fokine, and
a wunderkind dancer and choreographer, Vaslav
Nijinsky. Diaghilev's new ballets, including three
important Igor Stravinsky works, *The Firebird* in
1910, *Petrushka* in 1911 and *The Rite of Spring* in
1913, brought him worldwide fame and rocked the
foundations of ballet – as *The Rite*'s riotous first-
night audience confirmed (see page 58). He went
on to commission the likes of composers Ravel,
Richard Strauss, Prokofiev, Milhaud and Satie,
alongside designers such as Cocteau and Picasso,
building a unique body of work. When Diaghilev
died in 1929, his company disbanded, although
others sprang up sporting variants of its name.

As with modernism in other art forms, all the
formal rules of ballet were thrown into question. In
response to the parallel developments in music, ten-
sion and distortion became possible in movement;

angular silhouettes were permitted, and gravity could take the place of weightlessness. The concept of beauty no longer depended on concord and regularity.

In the US Martha Graham codified a system of dance based on contraction and release. She described being a dancer as 'permitting life to use you in a very intense way. Sometimes it is not pleasant. Sometimes it is fearful. But nevertheless it is inevitable.'

From the early years of the twentieth century, there has been little if any restriction on the subject-matter for dance. Once the natural state of the world could be experienced as random, destructive, cruel and absurd, the darkest of material could be interpreted in movement, as in any other art form.

Three women from Diaghilev's company were at the heart of British ballet: Marie Rambert, Alicia Markova, and Ninette de Valois. Marie Rambert (1888–1982) founded the Ballet Rambert in 1926, which later became the Rambert Dance Company. She seemed to have the gift of creating talented choreographers, with Frederick Ashton, Anthony Tudor and, later, Christopher Bruce all emerging from her company. This company that commissioned Poulenc and Prokofiev is also the company that danced Classic FM Composer in Residence Howard Goodall's *Eternal Light: A Requiem* in 2008.

Alicia Markova (1910–2004) was born Lilian Alicia Marks, and became one of the most influential dancers of the twentieth century. She danced with the Ballet Russes, the Rambert Dance Company, the Royal Ballet and many more. Not just the first British dancer to become a principal, but one of only two to be granted the status of *prima ballerina assoluta* – a rare honour bestowed on only the world's best dancers, whose service to ballet is seminal. Dame Margot Fonteyn (1919–1991) was the other – born Peggy Hookham, she went on to become President of the Royal Academy of Dance, and is also known for her famous on- and off-stage partnership with Rudolf Nureyev (1938–1993).

Ninette de Valois (1898–2001), born Edris Stannus, first came to prominence at Covent Garden in 1919 before opening her own academy in 1926. She commissioned the likes of Vaughan Williams and Bliss, with Constant Lambert making arrangements of existing works alongside. Her work with Lilian Baylis at the Old Vic Theatre led to the formation of the Vic–Wells company at the Sadler's Wells Theatre, which later became the Sadler's Wells Royal Ballet and then migrated to the Midlands to become the Birmingham Royal Ballet. Their collaboration also led to the establishment of the Royal Ballet Company, where de Valois remained director until her retirement in 1963, when Ashton, her chief choreographer, took over.

In 1970, Ashton was succeeded as director by choreographer Kenneth Macmillan (1929–1992), who had created many major works for the Royal Ballet and for the Deutsche Oper, Berlin. His choreography showed a willingness to explore the darker side of human nature and sexuality as well as demonstrating great wit and charm. This blend of darkness and light is similarly evident today in the work of Matthew Bourne and his company, Adventures in Moving Pictures. As well as creating completely new work, Bourne has also re-imagined existing classics with tenderness and inventiveness, revealing fresh delights in such warhorses as *The Nutcracker* and *Sleeping Beauty*, and staging a seminal all-male *Swan Lake*, in which the strength and muscularity of the corps de ballet and the questing sexuality of the prince were almost unbearably poignant.

In America, too, former Diaghilev dancers and choreographers were making waves. George Balanchine had been a Diaghilev favourite and was a close friend of Stravinsky. Balanchine opened the School of American Ballet in New York in 1934. Many would follow, creating a culture where ballet prospered, and leading to landmarks such as Copland's *Billy the Kid* for Ballet Caravan in 1938. Ballet Society became the New York City Ballet in 1948, eventually moving to its present home in the Lincoln Center sixteen years later.

Among contemporary American choreographers Mark Morris has developed an extraordinarily life-enhancing style of movement for his company. Technique is worn lightly as the sheer joy of being alive is conveyed to the audience. His material and his choice of soundtrack might sometimes be challenging, but his dancers' movement tends always towards the natural and, in his chorus works, a balance between the individual and the uniform that can be deeply moving.

Worldwide, ballet has continued to flourish, with many countries boasting a major state company and opera houses still supporting a separate dance company alongside an opera company working both independently and in tandem. Large companies usually maintain a repertoire that mixes familiar classics often dating from the nineteenth century and newer works, some even on the edge of becoming classics themselves.

You will never have to travel too far to find one of the great Tchaikovsky ballets or a standard work such as *Giselle* or *Coppélia*. Or you could discover whether one of the small, touring companies, pushing the envelope in choice of subject matter, presentation and sound track, could be to your taste.

three

Great Choreographers and Dancers

Choreographers are the bridge between music and dance, the designers of movement. Below we list a few who have caught the spirit of their age in sublime ballets and/or moved the genre in new and exciting directions.

Jean Balon (1676–1739)

Balon is one of the originals, a virtuoso dancer in the most prestigious ballet court of all, that of Louis XIV. It was he who appeared in the important work *Les Horaces* (see page 10) and was said to have been capable of light 'elastic' leaps. Indeed, the ballet term 'ballon' – the method of smooth ascent and descent when jumping – was said to have come from the other occasional spelling of his name.

Gaspare Angiolini (1731–1803)

An Italian dancer and choreographer, Angiolini's real name was Domenico Maria Angiolo Gasparini. Although he was born in Florence and died in Milan, his most famous work was performed in Vienna and St Petersburg. In the former, Angiolini's work with the composer Gluck was said to concentrate on 'the primacy of the dance', whilst in Russia, he was a crucial part of bringing realistic European ballet (*ballet d'action*) to the Imperial Theatre.

Auguste Bournonville (1805–1879)

Possibly the greatest Danish choreographer, Bournonville was born into a dancing family and trained in both Copenhagen and Paris. It was his period with the Royal Ballet of Copenhagen that saw him forge what is now known as the 'Bournonville school' or style, which itself drew on the earlier French masters. During this time, he was responsible for more than fifty ballets (all carefully preserved); they have enjoyed something of a renaissance since the mid-twentieth century. One of the delights of his work is that he collaborated with pretty much all the key Danish composers of his time, too, including Niels Gade and Hans Christian Lumbye.

Marius Petipa (1818–1910)

Petipa's choreography epitomises classical ballet at its best – weightless, delicate and exquisitely composed. After travelling the world as a principal dancer, Petipa settled in St Petersburg, forging a fruitful collaboration with Tchaikovsky and creating the legendary ballets that made his name: *Sleeping Beauty* (1890), *Don Quixote* (1869) and reworkings including *Giselle*, *Le Corsaire* and *La Sylphide*. His legacy has proved to be one of the most long lasting in all ballet.

Carlotta Grisi (1819–1899)

Grisi was one of the most celebrated dancers of her day. She gave the first ever performance of the title role in *Giselle* (1841), to music by Adolphe Adam, a role still beloved of ballerinas today. Such was the whirlwind praise and clamour surrounding her performance, her salary rocketed practically overnight, quadrupling in the space of three years.

Later she moved to St Petersburg but retired at the height of her popularity, to live for nearly fifty years in a villa in Geneva. Her cousins were the then-famous Giuditta and Giulia, two of Rossini's favourite singers.

Lev Ivanovich Ivanov (1834–1901)

Ivanov was the Russian dancer and choreographer who might be best remembered today for his *Dance of the Cygnets* from *Swan Lake*, part of the 'white' acts (the acts featuring the white swans) incorporated into Petipa's original choreography. He choreographed Tchaikovsky's ballet *The Nutcracker* when Petipa fell ill during rehearsals. Sadly, this dual relationship was to overshadow the rest of his life: as a choreographer, he personally felt he never stepped out from Petipa's shadow. But his genius is evident in the *Polovtsian Dances* from Borodin's opera *Prince Igor*, which seem to explode out into the audience.

Isadora Duncan (1877–1927)

Isadora Duncan was definitely a one-off. Born in America, she spent much of her life in Europe and the USSR. For her the Holy Grail was free, natural movement: 'the divine expression of the human spirit through the medium of the body's movement'. She substituted Grecian tunics and bare feet for corseted costumes and pointe shoes and cited the sea as her inspiration. 'Let them come forth with great strides,' she declared, 'leaps and bounds, with lifted forehead and far-spread arms, to dance.' Her thinking has perhaps been more influential than her choreography.

Michel Fokine (1880–1942)

Fokine was responsible for many of what is considered the classic-period Ballets Russes works: *The Firebird* (1910), *Petrushka* (1911) and *Daphnis et Chloé* (1912) among them. Prior to this period, his *Dying Swan* for Russian-born dancer Anna Pavlova in 1907 had made him one of the most talked-about choreographers of his time. Later, he settled in New York, occasionally overseeing revivals of some of his earlier successes. A famous letter to *The Times* in 1914 outlined his five principles for ballet choreography: don't use ready-made dance steps; dance must reinforce *drama*; be expressive from head to foot; use the entire corps de ballet as an expressive group, and always honour ballet's place in the arts, not submissive to either the music or the sets.

Tamara Karsavina (1885–1978)

Karsavina was one of the principal artists with Serge Diaghilev's legendary Ballet Russes. After having already danced almost every role with the Imperial Ballet, she was also the first to dance the title role in two of Stravinsky's iconic ballets, *Petrushka* and *The Firebird*, both alongside Nijinsky. After having spurned the advances of her choreographer, Michel Fokine, she married a British diplomat, Henry Bruce, and moved to Hampstead. Long after she finished dancing, she assisted in the work of Frederick Ashton, notably on a *La fille mal gardée* revival. Her former house in Hampstead is now the London Jewish Cultural Centre and contains a one-room exhibition in her memory.

Vaslav Nijinsky (1889–1950)

Nijinsky's is a name that will forever be linked to one of the most cataclysmic moments in dance history: his choreography for *The Rite of Spring* provoked a riot at the premiere in 1913. His strikingly modern movements, alongside the revolutionary music of Stravinsky, meant that dance would never be the same again. After an unceremonious break with Diaghilev in 1914, he attempted to start his

own company but was unsuccessful. Interned in
Hungary for some of the First World War, he later
settled in Switzerland, giving his last solo dance
performance in a hotel in St Moritz in 1919. In his
later years, following time in psychiatric hospitals,
he came to London, where he died in 1950.

Martha Graham (1893–1991)

Graham trained in Los Angeles with the Denishawn
Dancers before setting up her own school in 1927.
With some of the great American composers of the
twentieth century at her side, she became the leading exponent of modern dance in the US, with more
than 160 works to her name. The subject of more
than one painting by Andy Warhol – who was moved
by her work when he saw her dance in *Appalachian
Spring* – she is rightly accorded the epithet 'The
Mother of Modern Dance'.

Léonide Massine (1895–1979)

Massine, born Leonid Fyodorovich Myasin, learned
his trade in Moscow but shot to world attention
in Paris as principal choreographer of the Ballets
Russes, creating the ballets *Parade*, *Pulcinella*
and *La Boutique fantasque*. After spending time in

America and, later, with the Ballet Russe de Monte Carlo, he worked mostly in Europe, creating works with some of the world's greatest companies. Having worked in film (*The Red Shoes*, 1946, among others) he returned to the USSR in 1961 after an absence of fifty-seven years but did not settle. He was guest teacher at our own Royal Ballet for a short time.

Kurt Jooss (1901–1979)

Jooss was a German dancer and choreographer who initially studied at Stuttgart Academy of Music. It was there that he met the Hungarian dancer and notator Rudolf von Laban. Laban's influence was key to Jooss's formulation of German expression-ist dance movement, 'dance theatre' (*Tanztheater*). He established his noted Folkwang Tanztheater in Essen in 1927. Jooss fled the Nazis in 1933, set-tling in Dartington, England, where he reopened his dance company, but he returned to Essen to continue his work after the war.

Frederick Ashton (1904–1988)

Aside from having one of the greatest middle names of anyone in this book (Frederick William Malandaine Ashton), 'Sir Fred' was one of the greatest in the history of ballet choreography. Taught by Massine and Marie Rambert, he was the chief choreographer for the emerging Vic–Wells Ballet in the mid-twentieth century, going on to head up the Royal Ballet. He developed a uniquely British take on world-class choreography; a huge number of his dances are still in the repertoire of companies across the world, not least the Royal Ballet itself. His work with Margot Fonteyn (*Façade*, 1931; *Enigma Variations*, 1968; *A Month in the Country*, 1976) was among his most memorable.

George Balanchine (1904–1983)

Balanchine was a Russian-American, born George Balanchivadze, who learned the bedrock of his art at the Imperial Ballet School in his native St Petersburg. Today, he is remembered (revered, even) for his post-Russian period, however, as both the choreographer for the late-period Ballets Russes (working with the late-period Stravinsky, who became his lifelong friend) and as founder of the New York-based American Ballet Company (later American Ballet Caravan) from 1935. However, it was his work with the New York City Ballet from 1948 onwards that allowed him to create a truly great body of work, including his own *The Firebird* (1951), *Seven Deadly Sins* (1958) and *Variations* (1966).

Jerome Robbins (1918–1998)

Robbins bridged the gap between ballet and musical theatre. A multi-award-winning Broadway choreographer and director, his shows included *On the Town*, *Fiddler on the Roof* and *West Side Story*. In the 1970s and 1980s he worked extensively with the Joffrey Ballet and the New York City Ballet, which still includes the version of *The Firebird* he choreographed with Balanchine in its repertoire. Other ballets for the NYCB include *L'après-midi d'un faune*, *The Concert* and works to scores by Philip Glass and Charles Ives.

Merce Cunningham (1919–2009)

Cunningham was an associate of Martha Graham who pushed dance into abstract, avant-garde territory. His closest artistic collaboration was with the composer John Cage, his life partner, with whom he experimented with chance techniques, film and early computer technology. Other collaborations included those with the visual artists Robert Rauschenberg and Roy Lichtenstein and contemporary bands such as Radiohead.

Margot Fonteyn (1919–1991)

Fonteyn was born simple Peggy Hookham, in Reigate, Surrey, but went on to become Dame Margot Fonteyn de Arias DBE, one of the greatest classical ballet dancers of all time. From the corps of the Sadler's Wells school, she rose to become President of the Royal Academy of Dance. She will forever be linked in the public imagination with Russian defector Rudolf Nureyev, with whom she had an on- and off-stage partnership. When her death was announced, a Royal Opera House audience stood in silence.

Kenneth MacMillan (1929–1992)

If everyone is allowed to have a favourite, then I must confess that MacMillan is mine. He trained at Sadler's Wells and worked for Sadler's Wells Theatre Ballet (now Birmingham Royal Ballet) until becoming resident choreographer (later Director) at the Royal Ballet in 1965. It is his works with the Royal Ballet that are perhaps rightly considered his true masterpieces: anyone who has witnessed the tragic majesty of *Manon* (1974) or the sheer impact of *Romeo and Juliet* (1965), not to mention the mesmerising force of his reworking of *The Rite of Spring* (1962), cannot fail to appreciate his blistering creativity. He died, while backstage at the Royal Ballet, during a production of his *Mayerling* in 1992. The then-Director of the Opera House, Jeremy Isaacs, announced the news from the stage, mid-performance, asking the audience to 'please rise, bow your heads, and leave the theatre in silence'.

Rudolf Nureyev (1938–1993)

Possibly the world's most famous dancer of the last fifty years, Nureyev began his career as an amateur folk-dancer. After a period as soloist with the Kirov Ballet, he defected in 1961 while in Paris, joining the Royal Ballet in London soon after. It was here that his famous partnership with Margot Fonteyn began – at the time, he was twenty-four, she forty-two. One of only a handful of dancers to have crossed over into the wider public domain (he was in the 1971 *Morecambe and Wise Christmas Special* which also featured 'Andrew Preview') he went on to become Director of the Paris Opera Ballet.

Among contemporary choreographers whose work is still evolving in fascinating and enjoyable directions are Siobhan Davies (born in 1950), Mark Morris (born in 1956) and Matthew Bourne (born in 1960).

four

Composers of Ballet Music

There are some composers who wrote music for ballet scenarios and worked in collaboration with choreographers and dance companies. There are others whose music has been adopted by choreographers. Here is a brief selection of both.

Adolphe Adam (1803–1856)

Adam studied with Ferdinand Hérold, who composed the score for *La fille mal gardée*, and in turn taught Delibes, the composer of *Coppélia*. These days he is chiefly known for *Giselle* and *Le Corsaire*.

John Adams (born in 1947)

Both of Adams' operas *Nixon in China* and *The*

Death of Klinghoffer have included dance elements, both choreographed in their first productions by Mark Morris.

Samuel Barber (1910–1981)

Samuel Barber collaborated with Martha Graham for *The Cave of the Heart* (1946), a re-imagining of the Medea legend.

Ludwig van Beethoven (1770–1827)

Beethoven, with his ballet music for *Prometheus*, found himself present at one of the milestones in Romantic ballet. He wrote an overture, an introduction and then sixteen ballet movements.

Richard Rodney Bennett (1936–2012)

Richard Rodney Bennett provided Kenneth MacMillan with the score for his ballet *Isadora*, which focused on Isadora Duncan's private life – her relationships with theatre visionary Gordon Craig, poet Sergei Esenin and sewing-machine millionaire Paris Singer, and the deaths of her children to stillbirth and drowning. Bennett used pastiche for the dancer's public appearances, but his own voice for Isadora's personal life. The ballet also incorporated an actress speaking Duncan's polemical texts.

Leonard Bernstein (1918–1990)

Bernstein was a frequent collaborator with Jerome Robbins, notably for the musical *West Side Story*, but he also wrote *Fancy Free* for Robbins and the New York City Ballet as early as 1944 and *Dybbuk* for the same forces thirty years later.

Arthur Bliss (1891–1975)

Bliss was unusual as a composer in creating his own scenario for the ballet *Checkmate* in 1937, inspired by the Ballets Russes. The ballet, which shows chess pieces acting out violent and passionate human emotions, was choreographed by Ninette de Valois and was still in the repertoire of the Royal Ballet in 2011.

Alexander Borodin (1833–1887)

Borodin's unfinished opera *Prince Igor* provided choreographer Lev Ivanov with the opportunity of a lifetime with his exciting realisation of the *Polovtsian Dances*.

Benjamin Britten (1913–1976)

Britten wrote one full-length ballet, *The Prince of the Pagodas* (1957), for the Royal Ballet to a scenario by its choreographer, John Cranko. The first production had a mixed reception, but a later reworking by Kenneth MacMillan in 1989 with Darcey Bussell as Belle Rose met with more success. Britten also arranged a second set of Rossini movements, *Matinées musicales*, for Lincoln Kirstein, George Balanchine and the American Ballet, after their success with the ballet *Soirées musicales*, to Britten's earlier orchestral suite.

André Campra (1660–1744)

Having written several *tragédies en musique*, Campra is generally accorded the honour of having produced the first *opéra-ballet*, *L'Europe galante*, an examination of love in four cultures: France, Spain, Italy and Turkey.

Frédéric Chopin (1810–1849)

Chopin might not have set out to write ballet music, but his oeuvre has been continually mined for dance scores, including *Les Sylphides* (Michel Fokine), *A Month in the Country* (Frederick Ashton), and

The Concert and *Dances at a Gathering* (both by Jerome Robbins).

Aaron Copland (1900–1990)

That most American of composers, Aaron Copland, was another collaborator with Martha Graham, composing *Appalachian Spring* for her without a fixed scenario. The ballet celebrates the life of American pioneers in the nineteenth century. The orchestral suite has proved as successful as the ballet.

Claude Debussy (1862–1918)

L'après-midi d'un faune was composed in 1894 in response to a poem by Stéphane Mallarmé. Dreamy and languorous, ground-breaking in its uncertain tonality, the piece was seized on by Nijinsky to showcase his own charismatic sexuality.

Léo Delibes (1836–1891)

Delibes is cherished for two ballet scores, *Coppélia* and *Sylvia*. The latter was particularly admired by Tchaikovsky.

Alexander Glazunov (1865–1936)

The Seasons was the result of a commission swap

between two composers. Glazunov took on *The Seasons* for Petipa, while Riccardo Drigo picked up *Les Millions d'Arlequin*, also for Petipa. The ballets were premiered within three days of each other. Anna Pavlova, who danced Frost and Baccante in early performances, kept an abridged version in her touring company's repertoire for many years.

Christoph Willibald Gluck (1714–1787)

Gluck is an essential and revolutionary figure in the development of both opera and ballet, a champion of emotional truth in both genres.

Howard Goodall (born in 1958)

Classic FM's Composer-in-Residence was invited by London Musici and the Rambert Dance Company to compose a requiem for soloists, choir, orchestra and dancers. *Eternal Light: A Requiem* was the result, concentrating on the process of grief and acceptance, setting a mixture of sacred and secular texts and removing the concepts of sin and judgement from the more conventional requiem structure.

Charles Gounod (1818–1893)

Sometimes we should be grateful for rules. It was

unthinkable to stage an opera at the Paris Opera without a ballet. So Gounod added one for the Paris revival of his *Faust* in 1869. The opera (and the ballet) have been constantly performed around the world ever since.

George Frideric Handel (1685–1759)

Handel's London operas contain danced interludes and, like Chopin, his work has been frequently and successfully plundered by choreographers, perhaps most memorably by Mark Morris in his joyous ensemble piece, *L'Allegro, il Penseroso ed il Moderato*.

Scott Joplin (1868–1917)

Another joyous ensemble work is Kenneth MacMillan's *Elite Syncopations*, built around the ragtime music of Scott Joplin and his contemporaries. The jaunty music and inventive, upbeat choreography have displayed the skills of several generations of Royal Ballet stars over the years.

Aram Khachaturian (1903–1978)

Well represented in our 'Hall of Fame' and 'Download' sections is this Soviet Armenian composer, whose soaring themes, exciting rhythms and sensuous melodies have leant themselves so well to dramatic and romantic dance.

Franz Liszt (1811–1886)

For *Mayerling*, the most angst-ridden and romantic of his full-scale ballets, Kenneth MacMillan turned to the music of Franz Liszt, whose surface glitter can coat a much darker world. John Lanchbery, supreme ballet arranger and orchestrator for the Royal Ballet, produced an ideal score for the doom-laden love affair.

Jean-Baptiste Lully (1632–1687)

Lully was at the heart of Louis XIV's court and at the heart of the early stages of development of classical ballet. An accomplished dancer himself, he knew how to please his audience, having honed his skills with Molière's theatre group and then become the favourite of the king. He brought lively dances such as gavottes, minuets, rigaudons and sarabandes to the court to replace the more slow and stately styles. His contemporaries commented on the naturalness of his opera style, which inter-mingled recitative and aria, and something of this directness is present in his music for theatre and dance. His death is a cautionary tale for all conductors: on 8 January 1687, while conducting a performance of 'Te Deum' in l'Eglise du Couvent des Feuillants, Paris, he struck his toe with his conducting staff. An abscess later developed and, having refused his doctors' advice on amputation, Lully succumbed to gangrene some ten weeks later.

Jules Massenet (1842–1912)

Several of Massenet's works appear in our 'Downloads' section, but it is worth mentioning here that Kenneth MacMillan's score for *Manon*, while using Massenet's music, does not employ a single note of his opera of the same title.

Darius Milhaud (1892–1974)

Milhaud, fond of jazz and the saxophone, wrote his ballet *La Création du monde* based around African creation myths; it was designed by Ferdinand Léger. His surrealist *Le Boeuf sur le toit* was influenced by Brazilian music and choreographed by Jean Cocteau. Nowadays these ballet scores are more often found in the concert hall.

Francis Poulenc (1899–1963)

Diaghilev commissioned the score of *Les Biches* from Poulenc for the Ballets Russes. His *Gloria in G* was used by Kenneth MacMillan for the ballet *Gloria*, the choreographer's memorial to the dead of the First World War.

Sergei Prokofiev (1891–1953)

With Tchaikovsky and Stravinsky, Prokofiev is the third big Russian name when it comes to ballet scores, with *Cinderella* and *Romeo and Juliet* among others. *Cinderella* has been staged by a number of choreographers since its first production in 1945. The stepsisters are often danced by men – roles that Frederick Ashton and Robert Helpmann memorably made their own in the former's version of the ballet. Similarly, there are many versions of *Romeo and Juliet*, including those by Frederick Ashton, John Cranko, Kenneth MacMillan and Rudolf Nureyev. MacMillan's production rejuvenated Margot Fonteyn's career and marked the start of her partnership with Nureyev.

Henry Purcell (1659–1695)

Purcell wrote an immense amount of incidental

music for the theatre, for entertainments and spectacles involving dance. Mark Morris choreographed a ballet to Purcell's opera *Dido and Aeneas*, in an extraordinarily powerful piece of casting, dancing the dual role of Dido and the Sorceress himself.

Jean-Philippe Rameau (1683–1764)

The list of categories of Rameau's scores including music for dance sounds like Polonius' menu card for the players in *Hamlet*: *tragédies en musique, opéra-ballets, pastorales héroïques, comédies lyriques* and *comédies-ballets*. He was master of them all and with *Les Indes galantes* achieved a great success. However, later in life he was associated with the old guard and his artifice lost out to the new naturalness.

Maurice Ravel (1875–1937)

Ravel composed a substantial amount of music intended for ballet or appropriated for ballet by others. *Daphnis et Chloé* is his longest work. It was choreographed by Fokine for the Ballets Russes with Nijinsky and Tamara Karsavina as the lovers. Jerome Robbins created *Mother Goose* for New York City Ballet from the suite *Ma Mère l'oye*. The

New York company also staged George Balanchine's choreography to *Le Tombeau de Couperin*.

Camille Saint-Saëns

Among Saint-Saëns' vivid animal portraits (which include fossils and pianists in the line-up alongside lions and kangaroos) is the swan, scored originally for cello and two pianos. The long-breathed elegance and sweet sadness of the work proved ideal as a showcase for Anna Pavlova choreographed by Michel Fokine almost entirely *en pointe*. Pavlova performed *The Dying Swan* over 4000 times during her career.

Erik Satie (1866–1925)

Satie's *Parade* (1917) provided another *succès de scandale* for Diaghilev's Ballets Russes. The scenario was by Jean Cocteau, the choreographer was Léonide Massine and the set- and costume-designer Pablo Picasso. Everything was thrown at the stage. Satie brought music-hall, silent-film music and jazz; Cocteau added (frequently to Satie's chagrin) typewriters, foghorns and milk bottles – he also continued to work on the ballet right up until the first night, having had to travel to and from the Western Front, where he was officially fighting. Picasso found himself, at the last minute, painting a spiral design directly on to the body of a female acrobat whose role had been a late addition. And then there was the pantomime horse, with a cubist head and a mannequin rider attached to the back. On the first, uproarious night, the mannequin fell off. It was removed from subsequent performances.

Igor Stravinsky

Another inestimably large Russian name in the world of dance, with *The Rite of Spring*, *The Firebird*, *Petrushka* and *Pulcinella* among his major works. One smaller commission is less well known. In 1942 George Balanchine approached the composer with a slightly unusual request:

'I need you to write me a polka!' he barked.

'A-huh,' replied Stravinsky.

'For elephants,' came the rejoinder.

There was a pause.

'How old?' asked Stravinsky.

'Young,' Balanchine estimated.

Another pause.

'OK, if they're *very* young . . . I'll do it!'

And so the deal was done. Stravinsky provided Balanchine with music for his ballet for the Ringling Brothers Barnum and Bailey Circus and, specifically, a polka for elephants (yes, real, live elephants, fifty of them, all in pink tutus). *Circus Polka – for a Young Elephant* it was called and it ran, with the show, for 425 nights.

Pyotr Ilyich Tchaikovsky (1840–1893)

Attempting to define Tchaikovsky's remarkable gift for composing for dancers, David Brown points to his 'ability to create and sustain atmosphere: above all, a faculty for suggesting and supporting movement . . . animated by an abundant inventiveness, above all rhythmic, within the individual phrase'. He and his initial choreographers, Petipa and Ivanov, were indeed fortunate to be living at the same time, and between them brought Romantic ballet to its zenith. All three of Tchaikovsky's great ballet scores – *Swan Lake*, *Sleeping Beauty* and *The Nutcracker* – have been reworked by other choreographers since, including by Matthew Bourne, whose radical rethinking has revealed the central core of the works afresh.

Kurt Weill (1900–1950)

Weill's *Seven Deadly Sins* (1933) is unusual in being a 'sung ballet'. The central character, Anna, is divided into a singer and a dancer. The libretto, by Bertolt Brecht, turns bourgeois virtues into cynical sins. The hard-headed Anna I sings this inverted creed while soft-hearted Anna II dances the painful erosion of her 'goodness'. It demands virtuoso performance and sharp characterisation from both performers. It has attracted choreographers such as George Balanchine, Pina Bausch, Maurice Béjart and Kenneth MacMillan.

five

The Ballet Hall of Fame

It might come as a surprise that when you shake down the Classic FM Hall of Fame to separate music written for ballet, you are hard pressed to make up a top ten. Strictly disallowing anything that was not specifically written for a stand-alone ballet will actually yield only *nine* works. So, there is an odd one out in this line-up.

1. *Swan Lake* (1877)

Pyotr Ilyich Tchaikovsky

Swan Lake deserves its top place in our list if only because it's likely to be the first ballet most people will bring to mind. Its central premise is good versus evil; good swan Odette versus evil swan Odile (danced by the same ballerina in white and black tutus respectively). It was not an immediate success on its opening night, with choreography by Wenzel Reisinger (hence the choreography credits go principally to Marius Petipa and Lev Ivanov who put together a joint remake in 1895), but has acquired the status of perennial favourite almost ever since. In the UK, after a London premiere at the Hippodrome (just round the corner from the Classic FM studios), Diaghilev brought a Ballets Russes production in 1911, with Vaslav Nijinsky as evil sorcerer Von Rothbart. Tchaikovsky's original music was gradually superseded over a period of years by a medley of various 'fitting' pieces but was restored during the twentieth century. Recent years have seen a number of reinterpretations of the scenario and Matthew Bourne's all-male corps of swans. The 2010 film *Black Swan* features the ballet.

2. *Spartacus* (1956)

Aram Khachaturian

The story of the slave rebellion is familiar to anyone who, on a dull Sunday afternoon, has wept through Kirk Douglas, Jean Simmons *et al.* vying for the right to be called 'Spartacus'. This ballet version was produced for the Kirov Theatre in Leningrad (St Petersburg). Khachaturian had won the Lenin Prize with the score in 1954, having worked on it for some fifteen years. The famous *Onedin Line* moment, the delicious *Adagio of Spartacus and Phrygia*, comes in the second act, when Spartacus rescues his wife. Despite this fabulous moment, the ballet was not a success. A later production, at the Bolshoi, was even less successful. Nevertheless, Balanchine went on to create his own choreography, and the music survives courtesy of four separate, chronological ballet suites. As a result, despite the music proving to be some of Khachaturian's most popular, the complete ballet survives mainly in Russia (the Bolshoi, in particular) where it is known as *Spartak*, and in Khachaturian's native Armenia, at the Alexander Spendiarian State Opera and Ballet Theatre.

3. *The Nutcracker* (1892)

Pyotr Ilyich Tchaikovsky

It is difficult for us to imagine the popular excitement generated by classical music in years gone by. *The Nutcracker* is a case in point. With *Swan Lake* and *The Sleeping Beauty* already behind him, Tchaikovsky's musical stock, and Petipa's and Ivanov's reputation for choreography, meant a new ballet from these collaborators was simply not going to slip into the repertoire unnoticed. Posters began to appear around St Petersburg, announcing the forthcoming attraction: 'a fairy-tale ballet' was on its way, they declared, and for some time the glitterati were abuzz with little else but Tchaikovsky's and (eventually) Ivanov's new collaboration. (Petipa had to hand over the reins at the last minute, due to illness.) On the night, it was presented not on its own but in a double-bill. The other half of the evening was taken up with a Tchaikovsky one-act opera, *Iolanta*. The, quite simply, mad story line of *The Nutcracker*, based on an E. T. A. Hoffmann story (*Nussknacker und Mausekönig*) – boy meets evil uncle, girl meets soldier, boy/girl/soldier meet giant mouse – has proved popular with Christmas audiences ever since its first winter performance.

4. *Romeo and Juliet* (1938)

Sergei Prokofiev

There are some things in music and dance that make you do a double-take when you first hear them. For me, finding out that *West Side Story* was originally going to be called *East Side Story* was one such moment. Equally, when you look at the work in progress that was *Romeo and Juliet*, not long prior to the 1938 premiere, one thing *does* stand out: up until not long before opening night, the plot had been changed to include a happy ending.

Although the ballet was commissioned for a Soviet premiere at the Kirov Theatre, it was actually premiered in Brno until artistic issues could be sorted out within both the Kirov and the rival Bolshoi establishments. After 1940, the music did at least take off, while the ballet version eventually crossed over to the West some fifteen years later. Wanting to keep the music and the scenario but not the original choreography, the Royal Danish Ballet commissioned Frederick Ashton to produce his own choreography to Prokofiev's music. Stuttgart Ballet commissioned John Cranko to do the same thing. However, it is Kenneth MacMillan's 1965 reworking (premiered by Margot Fonteyn and Rudolf Nureyev as the lovers) that has lived on. One particular scene from the ballet, *Montagues and Capulets*, also known as *Dance of the Knights*, has proved particularly popular in some areas: it accompanies Sunderland FC footballers on to the pitch each week at home games, and is the title music for the television series *The Apprentice*.

5. *Sleeping Beauty* (1890)

Pyotr Ilyich Tchaikovsky

Tchaikovsky's second foray into ballet was eagerly anticipated. His was a huge name in music and Petipa was the supreme choreographer of the day, with an enormous body of work already under his belt. In their second collaboration, they achieved what many believe to be the high point of classical ballet in Russia. For Tchaikovsky, it was a great way to prove that ballet was something a great composer should be spending his time on (many were not so sure). For Petipa, he simply gave his best, from the stunning setting of the *Rose Adagio*, to the finale's grand *pas de deux*. From Russia, the ballet made very gradual progress around the world: Milan in 1896, New York in 1916 and a London Diaghilev production (although entitled *The Sleeping Princess*) in 1921 at the Alhambra Theatre (the Classic FM studios now sit on the site of the now long-gone Alhambra). Because of the expense involved in producing the ballet, it is one of those that occasionally see two or three companies combine to keep it in their joint repertoire. Indeed, Diaghilev's company could manage to keep only a shortened version permanently on the go.

6. *Appalachian Spring* (1944)

Aaron Copland

For those of us who listen to the variations on the Shaker hymn 'Simple Gifts' from Copland's music to *Appalachian Spring* and think how *perfectly* the composer captured the essence of that world and landscape, as winter melts into spring, a word of warning: all the guidance choreographer Martha Graham gave to Copland was that it was going to be on US pioneering themes.

His title for his music when it was sent across to her was the altogether less inspiring 'Ballet for Martha'. 'The fate of pieces is really rather curious,' he once said. 'You can't always figure out in advance exactly what's going to happen to them.' The rest, perhaps, is us filling in the gaps, in our minds.

The story, in the end, dealt with a newlywed American couple setting up home in the wilderness, with Copland, as he said, 'giving voice to the beauty of the region without knowing I was giving voice to it'. It was premiered at the Library of Congress in Washington DC, with Martha Graham in the lead role. Despite the title of the ballet being finalised long after Copland had composed most of it, this is a perfect fit of music and dance.

7. *The Rite of Spring* (1913)
Igor Stravinsky

It is possibly the most famous night in all ballet and it happened for a heady combination of reasons. Firstly, the impresario behind this and the rest of the Paris season, Serge Diaghilev, was very keen to have a *succès de scandale* on his hands. Secondly, Stravinsky was ready to go to new places in his music, especially when it came to creating a score for an extended fertility rite on stage. Finally, and perhaps most importantly, because the choreography of Vaslav Nijinsky was so revolutionary. Stravinsky's brutal rhythms were paralleled by the harsh, distorted shapes of the dancers' bodies. This was an evening when several new ideas exploded onto the ballet scene together at the Champs-Elysées Theatre, and the resulting furore was utterly predictable. The critic of the *Musical Times* wrote: 'The music of *Le Sacre du printemps* . . . baffles verbal description. To say that much of it is hideous as sound is a mild description . . . Practically, it has no relation to music at all, as most of us understand the word.'

A performance today is never going to invoke those first-night fireworks. In 1952, some thirty-nine years after the first performance, the original conductor, Pierre Monteux, returned to perform it again. The audience could not have been more different. A cacophony of noise? Totally unmusical? Non-music? Not at all. By now it was almost a standard in both the orchestral and ballet repertoire and the crowd loved it, greeting it with standing ovations. Monteux remarked, 'There was just as much noise last time, but the tonality was different!' Surprisingly, Monteux is also said to have told his biographer in old age, 'I did not like *The Rite* then. I have conducted it fifty times since. I do not like it now.'

However, certainly musically, *The Rite of Spring* (subtitled *Pictures of Pagan Russia in Two Parts*) will always remain a thought-provoking piece. Many reworkings have taken place over the years but my favourite remains that by Kenneth MacMillan. Anyone who saw Deborah Bull as The Chosen One some years ago might well agree with *The Times* review of its first night: 'Time and again,' it reported, 'Stravinsky's music, unaffectedly conducted by Mr Colin Davis, meets its match, as the choreography, with its blend of primitivism and modern jive, piles climax on climax.'

8. *The Firebird* (1910)
Igor Stravinsky

The story of *The Firebird* is a classic Russian fairy tale. It tells of Prince Ivan, who captures the magical Firebird, who then gives the prince a feather, which he can use to call her when he's in danger. And so he does, when he falls in love with Tsarevna, imprisoned by the evil Katschei. Thanks to the Firebird, Ivan is able to kill Katschei and marry his beloved Tsarevna. This scenario was never meant to go to Stravinsky. The idea was to have music composed by Lyadov – a fine composer who, sadly for him but thankfully for us, experienced a severe case of 'composer's block'. With Stravinsky at the helm, the ballet has become one of the world's greatest. Stravinsky, a mere stripling of twenty-seven, went from a precocious young thing to a worldwide sensation. Up until this point, too, the choreographer

Michel Fokine was principally known as the man behind Pavlova's *The Dying Swan*. From here on, he was one of the kings of choreography and toured the world. Incidentally, if you ever get to see the New York City Ballet version, with choreography by Balanchine and Jerome Robbins, they still use the wonderful Marc Chagall sets and costumes, which are well worth the entrance fee alone.

9. *L'Après-midi d'un faune* (1912)
Claude Debussy

Here it is, our odd one out. Strictly speaking, not composed for ballet but written by Debussy some eighteen years before Nijinsky choreographed the piece for himself. Nevertheless, as the composer was still alive at the time of the 1912 premiere, and as it was a Ballets Russes premiere, I've allowed it in.

The *Prélude à l'après-midi d'un faune* had gone a long way to establishing its composer's name. Then, as now, it was largely agreed to be a ten-minute orchestral piece that changed the face of orchestral music. When Nijinsky was casting around for new inspiration, it was the 'Greek vase' quality he felt he could hear in the music that inspired him. The set designer for the ballet, Léon Bakst, produced some of his most delightful work for this piece and, as a result of his and Debussy's influence, the dancers moved as if in 'relief', in profile, on the front of a Greek vase. *L'Après-midi d'un faune* came to be seen as one of the first truly *modern* ballets.

10. *Coppélia* (1870)

Léo Delibes

Here's a ballet based on E. T. A. Hoffmann's *Der Sandmann* – as is part of Offenbach's *The Tales of Hoffmann*. In the ballet version, Dr Coppelius (a cousin of Pygmalion and Frankenstein) creates a doll with a soul: a living doll. Franz, who deep down loves Swanilde, is infatuated by the doll. Eventually, realising his folly, he returns to Swanilde, and all is well. This intriguing tale, combined with the seemingly effortlessly attractive music of Delibes, has meant that, despite it being nearly some 150 years old, *Coppélia* is still firmly in the repertoire of many companies across the globe. Petipa's choreography superseded Arthur Saint-Leon's original and other versions have been presented since. Interestingly enough, it was a tradition of the ballet, in France at least, that the part of Franz was played *en travesti*

– that is, by a woman. This continued up until the Second World War. In the 1970s, Balanchine reworked a version for the New York City Ballet, maintaining Petipa's steps for Act II, while rechoreographing Acts I and III.

The Concert (1956)

Frédéric Chopin

I've included one more. It wasn't voted into the Hall of Fame. Neither is it, usually, included on the average bucket list of great ballets. I've included it, though, because it is, in my opinion, the perfect introduction to ballet. If you want to take someone along to ballet for the first time in the desperate hope that they will love it as much as you do, then Jerome Robbins' *The Concert* is, I think, the one. (It is usually included as one in a triple-bill so, with luck, you'll get another couple of corkers too.)

It is set to an all-Chopin piano score (the pianist plays live on stage as the dancers dance around) and, as the title suggests, is centred largely around a concert. Its use of humour combined with truly inventive, world-class choreography makes it, for me, a must-see on any new ballet lover's list.

six

50 Ballet Tracks to Download

All these tracks can be found as a downloadable play-list on our website at ClassicFM.com/handyguides.

Tchaikovsky: *Swan Lake*

1   Act I, No. 2: *Valse*
2   Act I, No. 9: *Finale: Andante*
3   Act II, No. 10: *Scène: Moderato*
4   Act II, No. 13d: *Danse des petits cygnes: Allegro moderato*
5   Act III: *Pas de deux – Introduction: Moderato; Variations I and II; Coda*

This gives you a rounded take on *Swan Lake* across its three acts, from the sumptuous and often explosive Act I corps de ballet *Waltz* right through the 'must-have' *Dance of the Cygnets*, to the showpiece *Pas de deux* in Act III.

Prokofiev: *Romeo and Juliet*

6 Act I, No. 12: *Masks*
7 Act I, No. 13: *Dance of the Knights*
8 Act III, No. 38: *Romeo and Juliet*

Three lovely moments from one of my favourite ballets. (I shall never forget seeing Viviana Durante and Irek Mukhamedov as my *favourite* Romeo and Juliet.) *Masks* is a cheeky little thing with Romeo and Benvolio, uninvited guests at a Capulet ball, both wearing masks. The *Dance of the Knights* (aka *Montagues and Capulets*) is possibly the highlight of the ballet for many. Well staged (and I can only further recommend the Kenneth MacMillan realisation of it – simply stunning) it can be an almost hard-to-recover-from scene-stealer.

Delibes: *Coppélia*

9 Act I, No. 3: *Mazurka*
10 Act I, No. 5: *Ballade de l'épi*
11 Act I, No. 8: *Csárdás (Danse hongroise); Sortie*
12 Act III: *Fête de la cloche: 7a La Paix*

No download collection would be complete without

something from the perennial *Coppélia*. Here are the roister-doister Act I *Mazurka* (possibly the musical highlight of the ballet), the more or less following *Ballade de l'épi*. The *épi*, or 'ear', is an ear of wheat: Coppélia the doll shakes the ear of wheat by her head in the belief that, if it rattles, this means Franz loves her: well, I guess it's as sure a method as any. There is also the majestic *Csárdás* and the last-act grand *Pas de deux 'La Paix'*, which, ever since the role of Franz stopped being played by a woman, has probably become the dance highlight of most productions.

Tchaikovsky: *Sleeping Beauty*
13 Act I: *Adagio ('Rose Adagio')*
14 Act I: *Valse des fleurs*
15 Act II: *Panorama*

For many, the *Rose Adagio* is not just the highlight of *Sleeping Beauty* but the highlight of all ballet, a perfect mix of Petipa's choreography and one of Tchaikovsky's best tunes.

It is so called because the dance involves Princess Aurora being presented to four suitors, each of whom presents her with a rose (and, incidentally, each of which she rejects). While we might be sitting there, rapt in wonder at the beauty of the dance (I once saw the now-*Strictly* Darcey Bussell take people's breath away with the sheer perfection of execution), it is perhaps good to remember that, for the ballerina, this is one of the hardest routines in all ballet.

The *Valse des fleurs* is a must-have in any ballet collection.

Prokofiev: *Cinderella*
16 *Duet of the Prince and Cinderella*
17 *Waltz-Coda*
18 *Midnight*
19 *Waltz*

This is a lovely set of excerpts, mainly from the end of Act II of *Cinderella*. Just prior to this, there has been a cute self-reference by Prokofiev to his own music: he has Cinderella taste 'the kingdom's finest delicacy', namely three oranges, complete with musical quotations from his *The Love of Three Oranges*. Nice. Then the Prince whisks Cinders off into the garden (for the duet) before her mad rush, final waltz and all, to get back home before midnight.

Finally, here too is the exquisite, shifting slow *Waltz*, taken from the moment that the Prince has just managed to fit the slipper on to Cinderella's foot. This is Prokofiev capturing perfectly that feeling of total, all-consuming love. Stop me now, before I well up.

Chopin: *Les Sylphides*

20 *Prélude*

21 *Nocturne*

22 *Valse*

The music for *Les Sylphides* was originally called *Chopiniana* when Glazunov first orchestrated a selection of Chopin's piano music for the concert hall in 1893. Although Chopin was long gone when the ballet, choreographed by Fokine for the Ballets Russes, was premiered in 1909 and he had never intended his music for the ballet, it fits beautifully. *Les Sylphides* is possibly the classic *ballet blanc* with the entire corps de ballet in white, below-the-knee ballet skirts rather than tutus.

Ferdinand Hérold arr. John Lanchbery: *La fille mal gardée*

23 Act 1: *Clog Dance* (Peter Ludwig Hertel)

The *Clog Dance* is the comic masterpiece, often danced Widow Twanky-style by a veteran of the company, and which is often wrongly ascribed to Hérold himself. It's a fair old mix-up. Several people had written music for *La fille mal gardée* over the years and when John Lanchbery was looking to rearrange the music for the new Frederick Ashton production in 1959, he went almost exclusively for the Hérold music. But the one piece he rejected was the *Clog Dance*: for this he reorchestrated the music from the Hertel ballet score – and how right he was too.

Massenet *et al.*: *L'Histoire de Manon*
24 *Le dernier Sommeil de la Vièrge (The Last Sleep of the Virgin)*

The opening moments of a 1974 Kenneth MacMillan classic for the Royal Ballet, *L'Histoire de Manon*, which uses a Massenet remnant, *The Last Sleep of the Virgin*, the only part of his epic oratorio *La Vierge* to have survived. Exquisite.

Stravinsky: *The Firebird*
25 *Lullaby of the Firebird*

A softer moment from a fierce ballet. Firstly, the bassoon and oboe undulations in the first-act *Lullaby* give way to stunning string music for the Firebird herself. It's a wonderful moment in the ballet, as she flits across the stage, seemingly lighting it up as she does.

Gounod: *Faust*

26 *Adagio*

The delicious ballet music from Gounod's opera *Faust* (at the time it was to play at the Paris Opera, you couldn't perform an opera there if it didn't contain a ballet) is a pearl, danced, in the opera, on Walpurgis Night – 30 April.

Johann Strauss II, orch. Roger Desormière: *The Blue Danube*

27 *Andantino: Tempo di valse*

Johann Strauss II wrote only one ballet – *Cinderella*. It was discovered only after he died and Mahler famously refused to stage the completed work in 1900 when he was running the Vienna Court Opera. However, lots of his music has been used in ballets – *The Blue Danube* was choreographed by Massine in 1924.

Johann Strauss II: *Voices of Spring*

28 *Waltz: Voices of Spring*

Ashton choreographed *Voices of Spring* (*Frühlingsstimmen*) for a 1977 production of Strauss's *Die Fledermaus* for the Royal Opera House, replacing one of the numbers on the Act II ball scene. It has since had an independent life as a *pas de deux*, particularly in galas.

Rossini arr. Britten: *Matinées musicales*
29 *Nocturne*

The second set of Britten's Rossini arrangements was composed at the request of Lincoln Kirstein and the American Ballet Company to form a double-bill in tandem with his *Soirées musicales*, both choreographed by George Balanchine.

Tchaikovsky: *Souvenir d'un lieu cher*
30 *Souvenir d'un lieu cher*

Russian choreographer Alexei Ratmansky adopted Tchaikovsky's fabulous *Souvenir* for violin and piano for his ballet of the same name.

Delibes: *Sylvia*
31 *Pizzicati*

No collection is complete without something from *Sylvia* and this is a classic moment. Sylvia, incidentally, was written not long before Tchaikovsky's *Swan Lake* and it is lucky Tchaikovsky hadn't seen Delibes' score before he penned his own classic. When he finally did, he is quoted as saying. 'I was ashamed. If I had known this music early then, of course, I would not have written *Swan Lake*.'

Glazunov: *The Seasons*
32 *Autumn*
This is the moment the leaves rain down from this 1900 ballet choreographed by Petipa.

Massenet: *Scènes alsaciennes*
33 *Dimanche matin*
The rarely performed *Scènes alsaciennes* is one of Massenet's many orchestral suites – perhaps most heartfelt as a hymn to the 'lost' (to France, at least) region of Alsace.

Massenet: *Le roi de Lahore*
34 *Entr'acte Act V; Adagio and Waltz; Ballet Act III*
Paris Opera rules applied to Massenet's opera *The King of Lahore*, and so he added the obligatory ballet.

Adam: *Le Corsaire*
35 *Corsaires' Bacchanale*
Le Corsaire is a Petipa classic, first presented at the

Paris Opera in 1856, and the *Bacchanale* (sometimes spelt *Bacchanal*) is one of those showpiece moments.

Czibulka: *Love's Dream After the Ball*
36 *Love's Dream After the Ball*

Love's Dream After the Ball was one of Anna Pavlova's signature dances. As one critic lucky enough to have seen her dance said at the time, 'Slender and graceful as a reed, and as supple, with the ingenuous face of a girl of southern Spain, ethereal and light, she seemed like a fragile and elegant Sèvres statuette . . . Here was something individual, something that was not learned at school.'

Minkus: *La Bayadère*
37 *La Bayadère*

An extract from Ludwig Minkus's score for the trials and tribulations of a temple dancer and her warrior lover. Minkus was Petipa's regular composer of choice.

Ponchielli: *La Gioconda*
38 *Dance of the Hours*

This short ballet section from Amilcare Ponchielli's

opera, *La Gioconda*, is a whistle-stop dance through twenty-four hours in a series of solo and ensemble dances. It was immortalized in *Fantasia*, danced by animated ostriches, hippos, elephants and alligators.

Adam: *Giselle*
39 *Grand Pas de deux*
Giselle is said to be the ballet that has inspired more young girls to become ballerinas than any other. This stunning *Grand pas de deux* is one good reason why. (See also No. 41 below.)

Saint-Saëns: *The Carnival of the Animals*
40 *The Swan*
Saint-Saëns' *Carnival of the Animals* became a ballet in 1943 for the Rambert Dance Company, and featured a Victorian child who encountered all the animals in turn.

Adam: *Giselle*
41 *Danse des vignerons – Pas seul – Peasant Pas de deux*
The villagers' dance (sometimes *marche*), the solo and the so-called *Peasant Duet* from the first act of *Giselle*.

Youmans orch. Shostakovich: *Tahiti Trot*
42 *Tahiti Trot*

Shostakovich won a bet by taking less than an hour to reorchestrate Vincent Youmans' 'Tea for Two' from the musical *No, No, Nanette*. It was subsequently used as an entr'acte in Shostakovich's ballet *The Golden Age*.

Khachaturian: *Masquerade Suite*
43 *Waltz*

Khachaturian put together a suite from his incidental music to Lermontov's play, the last production at Moscow's Vakhtangov Theatre before the invasion of the USSR by Germany.

Khachaturian: *Gayaneh*
44 *Adagio*

Khachaturian had a bit of a knack for ballet. *Gayaneh* dates from 1942, when it was premiered at the Kirov in Leningrad (St Petersburg). Eschewing the hair-raising *Sabre Dance*, we've plumped for soulful *Adagio*, which also caught the ear of director Stanley Kubrick, in his film *2001: A Space Odyssey*.

Khachaturian: *Spartacus*

45 *Adagio of Spartacus and Phrygia*

Another Adagio from Khachaturian – the love *Adagio* from *Spartacus*, composed twenty-odd years later than *Gayaneh*'s, has – it's fair to say – achieved more fame.

Tchaikovsky: *The Nutcracker*

46 Act I: *March*

47 Act II: *Trepak (Russian Dance)*

48 Act II: *Dance of the Reed Pipes*

49 Act II: *Waltz of the Flowers*

50 Act II: *Dance of the Sugar Plum Fairy*

For some, this ballet is like the Queen's Speech: without it, Christmas wouldn't be Christmas. This is a fun five-some of favourites that would be fabulous in any collection.

seven

Where To See Ballet

UK

Royal Ballet

Royal Opera House, Covent Garden, London

www.roh.org.uk

Founded by Ninette de Valois in 1931 and presenting a mix of classical ballets and new works from today's choreographers, all of them world class. Directed by Kevin O'Hare, the company's current stars, such as Carlos Acosta, continue the stunning work of the founding dancers, including *prima ballerina assoluta* Margot Fonteyn. Needless to say, the building, and sometimes the price of a ticket, is out of this world.

Scottish Ballet

Tramway Arts Centre, Glasgow

www.scottishballet.co.uk

Founded in 1957 in Bristol as Western Theatre Ballet, the company moved to Scotland in 1969, staging works in both the Glasgow Theatre Royal and its recent new venue, the Tramway Arts Centre, as well as touring. It has a broad repertoire of classics, modern classics and new commissions.

English National Ballet

Markova House, London

www.ballet.org.uk

In the company's own words: 'a bold company of ambitious dancers, choreographers, costumiers, musicians and designers. We perform ballet *anywhere.*' The Artistic Director and lead principal is the former Royal Ballet star Tamara Rojo and the wide repertoire encompasses everything from classical ballet, through Ballet Russes standards to recent commissions.

Birmingham Royal Ballet

Thorp Street, Birmingham

www.brb.org.uk

Founded originally as the Sadler's Wells Theatre Ballet and now independent of, although retaining strong links with, the Royal Ballet, with HM The Queen as its Patron and HRH The Prince of Wales as its President. One of the world's leading large-scale international dance companies, aiming for 'outstanding creativity and artistic excellence'.

Northern Ballet

West Park Centre, Leeds

www.northernballet.com

Established in 1969 by Canadian-born Laverne Meyer, the company's period under former Royal Ballet star Christopher Gable (up until 1998) gained it a worldwide reputation. Today David Nixon is in his twelfth season as Artistic Director and that reputation is very much intact.

Rambert Dance Company

Chiswick High Road, London

www.rambert.org.uk

The name is the giveaway here, the key to a history stretching back to 1926. Founded by one of the greats, Marie Rambert, the company continues to stage bold new works, fresh and vital, yet infused with the heritage of the UK's oldest dance company. Classic FM's own Howard Goodall recently worked with the company's Artistic Director, Mark Baldwin, to produce the ballet premiere of his work, *Eternal Light: A Requiem*.

Scottish Dance Theatre

Dundee Rep Theatre, Tay Square, Dundee

www.scottishdancetheatre.com

If you like your dance a little more contemporary, this is for you. Under Artistic Director Fleur Darkin, the company is committed to presenting 'daring' works by the 'most exciting' choreographers. One recent work featured 10 dancers, 80 bamboo sticks and 120 ropes – and by the end of the evening, the dancers had built a shelter.

Siobhan Davies Dance

St George's Road, London

www.siobhandavies.com

'An investigative contemporary arts organisation', as its own description has it, the company was founded by one of the London Contemporary Dance Company's leading dancer–choreographers (and sometime Rambert veteran) Siobhan (often known as Sue) Davies. Genuinely at the cutting edge of contemporary dance.

Austria
Wiener Staatsballett
www.wiener-staatsoper.at

The Wiener Staatsballett is currently directed by Maniel Legris, Paris-born former star of the l'Opéra ballet. No sooner had he arrived than he brought not only a Rudolf Nureyev production of *Don Quixote* but also a little mini-season devoted to Jerome '*West Side Story*' Robbins. He has a corps of seventy-odd dancers and numerous soloists and guest soloists. Try not to be distracted not only by the amazing building but also by the thought of people like Mahler conducting here.

Salzburger Ballett
www.salzburger-landestheater.at

Denmark
Royal Danish Ballet
www.kglteater.dk

The Danes have a long history of ballet. Theirs is

the world's third-oldest company, based in the capital Copenhagen with roots traceable back to 1748 (the Royal Danish Ballet School proudly boasts a 1771 birthday, which is far earlier than our Royal Ballet School). Not surprisingly, the company stages an extensive range of classical ballets but also prides itself on commissioning the finest choreographers of the day, at both the grand old Kongelige Theater and the much more modern Royal Danish Playhouse not far away.

Danish Dance Theatre

www.danskdanseteater.dk

Peter Schaufuss Ballet

www.schaufuss.com

Finland

Finnish National Ballet

www.opera.fi

A twentieth-century ballet company employing some seventy or so dancers, majoring on the classical repertoire in seasons that regularly sell out. Kenneth Greve, formerly of New York City Ballet, has recently re-signed his contract to continue as its Artistic Director up until 2018.

France

Opéra national de Paris

www.operadeparis.fr

Where it all began. Today there are 154 dancers, 18 principal dancers, and 14 prima ballerinas performing a massive repertoire of most of the major Romantic and Classical ballets plus lots more over a season that features some 180 performances. Tickets, which can be pricy, sometimes sell out in hours.

Ballet d'Europe

www.balletdeurope.org

Ballet de Lorraine

www.ballet-de-lorraine.com

Ballet du Nord

www.balletdunord.fr

Ballet de l'Opéra du Rhin

www.operanationaldurhin.fr

Les Ballets de Monte-Carlo

www.balletsdemontecarlo.com

Centre chorégraphique national de Grenoble

www.gallotta-danse.com

Centre chorégraphique national d'Orléans

www.josefnadj.com

Germany

Hamburg Ballet

www.hamburgballett.de

Hailing from Milwaukee, Wisconsin, John Neumeier is the guiding light of Hamburg Ballet and has been for some forty years. His amazing tenure has seen him produce just about every ballet under the sun and, in 2011, he even founded the elite National Youth Ballet, also based in Hamburg. His speciality is tradition (the 2014–15 season, for example, features a *Giselle*, a *Nutcracker*, and a *Romeo and Juliet*) but with a modern framework – and it's certainly been successful.

Ballett Nürnberg

www.staatstheater-nuernberg.de

Bayerisches Staatsballett (Munich)

www.staatsoper.de/staatsballett

Leipzig Ballet

www.oper-leipzig.de

Semperoper Dresden

www.semperoper.de

Staatsballett Berlin

www.staatsballett-berlin.de

Stuttgart Ballet

www.stuttgart-ballet.de

Norway

Norwegian National Ballet

www.operaen.no

There are not far short of sixty dancers in the company, which is, taken in conjunction with the National Opera, by far the biggest performing arts organisation in the country, run from the new, ocean-side Opera House – a stunning building not without its detractors. Ticket prices can reach £320.

Portugal

National Ballet of Portugal

www.cnb.pt

Founded in 1977, Portugal's National Ballet, resident in the 'blue box' of Teatro Camões, looking
out across the bay of Lisbon, is currently in the
hands of Artistic Director Luisa Taveira, a gradu-
ate of London's Royal Ballet School and founder of
the contemporary dance group Grupo Experimental
de Bailado do Porto. The company numbers over
fifty dancers and soloists, presenting both traditional
Balanchine and Bournonville productions as well
as works by Portugal's finest choreographers, such
as Olga Roriz.

Spain

Ballet Nacional de España

balletnacional.mcu.es

Antonio Najarro is possibly one of the only artistic
directors of a national ballet company who would be
recognised, even mobbed, if he walked down a public street. He is one of the country's most famous
flamenco dancers. He also has a nice sideline in
figure-skating choreography, helping some of the
world's international and Olympic champions to

victory. While ice might not feature in his ballets, the flamenco influence is strong.

Sweden

Royal Swedish Ballet

www.operan.se

This is one of the oldest companies in Europe, founded in 1773 just a couple of years after its Danish counterpart. Its Artistic Director is Johannes Ohman, formerly of the Gothenburg Ballet, where he was sometimes seen as too traditional, although now that he is at the Royal, some detractors have complained that he is too contemporary. No doubt this is partly because he has maintained a healthy modern repertoire alongside the classical favourites. The company's soloists also make up the forward-looking group Stockholm 59°North (www.stockholm59north.com), formed in 1997 by Royal Court dancer Madeleine Onne.

Switzerland

Ballet Zurich

www.opernhaus.ch

One of the newest artistic directors with an international ballet company, Christian Spuck took over Ballet Zurich only in 2012, but has continued its tradition of classical and innovative ballet programming. At the time of writing, four shows in the current season are his own choreographies, with American master William Forsythe and Balanchine among the rest. Two short seasons of young choreographers are also featured.

Béjart Ballet Lausanne

www.bejart.ch

Grand Théâtre de Genève

www.geneveopera.ch

US

New York City Ballet

www.nycballet.com

Any ballet company that could boast George Balanchine as its founder – and Jerome Robbins as former co-Ballet Master in Chief – is probably a must-experience, and the New York City ballet is exactly that. From its wonderful home in the Lincoln Center's David H. Koch Theater, it runs a stunning programme across twenty-one weeks of the year. Current supremo Peter Martins has been there since the Balanchine days, first as a dancer and now as Ballet Master in Chief. If you have young ones, the Family Saturdays, at just $20, are a bargain.

Mark Morris Dance Group (New York)

www.markmorrisdancegroup.org

Over in Brooklyn, you might like to find a night for the Mark Morris Company. Formerly resident in Brussels and sought after around the world, Mark Morris productions have included *Falling Down Stairs*, a work choreographed around a performance of Bach's Third Cello Suite by Yo-Yo Ma. You will not see Mark Morris perform himself but his productions are always world class.

American Ballet Theatre (New York)

www.abt.org

Houston Ballet

www.houstonballet.org

Isadora Duncan Dance Company (New York)

www.isadoraduncan.org

Merce Cunningham Dance Company (New York)

www.mercecunningham.org

San Francisco Ballet

www.sfballet.org

Washington Ballet

www.washingtonballet.org

About Classic FM

If this series of books has whetted your appetite to find out more, one of the best ways to discover what you like about classical music is to listen to Classic FM. We broadcast a huge breadth of classical music 24 hours a day across the UK on 100–102 FM, on DAB digital radio, online at ClassicFM.com, on Sky Channel 0106, on Virgin Media channel 922 and on FreeSat channel 721. You can also download the free Classic FM App, which will enable you to listen to Classic FM on your iPhone, iPod, iPad, Blackberry or Android device.

As well as being able to listen online, you will find a host of interactive features about classical music, composers and musicians on our website, ClassicFM.com. When we first turned on Classic FM's transmitters more than two decades ago, we changed the face of classical music radio in the UK for ever. Now, we are doing the same online.

The very best way to find out more about which pieces of classical music you like is by going out and hearing a live performance by one of our great British orchestras for yourself. There is simply no substitute for seeing the whites of the eyes of a talented soloist as he or she performs a masterpiece on stage only a few feet in front of you, alongside a range of hugely accomplished musicians playing together as one.

Classic FM has a series of partnerships with orchestras across the country: the Bournemouth Symphony Orchestra, the London Symphony Orchestra, the Orchestra of Opera North, the Philharmonia Orchestra, the Royal Liverpool Philharmonic Orchestra, the Royal Northern Sinfonia and the Royal Scottish National Orchestra. And don't forget the brilliant young musicians of the National Children's Orchestra of Great Britain and of the National Youth Orchestra of Great Britain. To see if any of these orchestras have a concert coming up near you, log onto our website at ClassicFM.com and click on the 'Concerts and

Events' section. It will also include many other classical concerts – both professional and amateur – that are taking place near where you live.

Happy listening!

About the Author

Tim Lihoreau is the presenter of Classic FM's *More Music Breakfast*, which can be heard every weekday morning between 6 a.m. and 9 a.m. Previously Tim presented the programme at the weekends, before moving to weekdays and taking over the reins of the UK's most listened-to classical music breakfast show in 2012. His career as a presenter, which stretches back more than a decade, has operated in tandem with his role as Classic FM's creative director and has seen him presenting programmes for the station at all hours of the day and night. He has been responsible for writing and producing many of Classic FM's biggest programmes and he has won a string of major accolades on both sides of the Atlantic at the Radio Academy Awards, the

New York International Radio Festival and the Arqiva Commercial Radio Awards.

Tim studied Music at the University of Leeds and worked as a professional pianist and in the classical record industry before making the move to Classic FM as a producer in 1993. He is the author of fifteen books, including *The Incomplete and Utter History of Classical Music*, which accompanied the award-winning Classic FM series of the same name, presented by Stephen Fry. Alongside his wife, Tim runs three amateur choirs in his home village in Cambridgeshire and regularly plays his local church organ.

Index

Index